STATIONS OF THE CROSS BOOK

Peter Cullen

McCRIMMON
Great Wakering Essex England

First published in Great Britain in 1981 by
MAYHEW McCRIMMON LTD
Great Wakering Essex England

ISBN 0 85597 304 8

Cover design and Layout Nick Snode
Illustrations The Benedictine Nuns
Printed by Mayhew McCrimmon Printers Ltd

Introduction

The fourteen Stations of the Cross are traditionally a lenten devotion. I thought it might be of value to combine our celebration of them with the eucharist. Accepting that the Stations are penitential in nature and are easily based upon scripture I decided to use them as the penitential rite and liturgy of the word in preparation for the eucharist; thus emphasising that the suffering and death of Jesus make sense only in the light of the resurrection.

I have often found that a scriptural meditation on the Stations of the Cross has brought me to a more thorough examination of conscience and a deeper awareness of the need for God's healing love. After choosing a scripture reading for each Station I then composed an examination of conscience using the familiar 'Lord, have mercy' response from the penitential rite at Mass. Finally, making aware the redemptive aspect of Christ's sufferings, I added a positive prayer asking for God's healing in our lives.

I offer these meditations in the hope that the power of God's love experienced through the suffering, death and resurrection of Jesus may help others to turn again in response to the call he makes to each of us.

The power of these meditations is reflected in the series of posters by the Benedictine Sisters which happily contain the two additional scripturally based Stations: 'Jesus speaks to his mother from the cross' and 'Jesus is risen'.

P.C.

1 Jesus is Condemned to Death

(Matthew 27: 20–26)

The chief priests and the elders, however, had persuaded the crowd to demand the release of Barabbas and the execution of Jesus. So when the governor spoke and asked them, 'Which of the two do you want me to release for you?' they said, 'Barabbas'. 'But in that case,' Pilate said to them, 'what am I to do with Jesus who is called Christ?' They all said, 'Let him be crucified!'. 'Why?' he asked, 'What harm has he done?' But they shouted all the louder, 'Let him be crucified!'. Then Pilate saw that he was making no impression, that in fact a riot was imminent. So he took some water, washed his hands in front of the crowd and said. 'I am innocent of this man's blood. It is your concern.' And the people, to a man, shouted back 'His blood be on us and on our children!'. Then he released Barabbas for them. He ordered Jesus to be first scourged and then handed over to be crucified.

Lord, for the times I have washed my hands of my responsibilities,
Lord, have mercy.
Lord, for the times I fail to have the courage to do what I know is right,
Christ, have mercy.
Lord, for the times I blame others for my actions,
Lord, have mercy.
Lord, heal my memories of those occasions when I have been wrongly accused, and help me forgive those who have judged me unjustly.

2 Jesus Takes up his Cross

(Matthew 27: 27–31)

The governor's soldiers took Jesus with them into the Praetorium and collected the whole cohort round him. There they stripped him and made him wear a scarlet cloak, and having twisted some thorns into a crown they put this on his head and placed a reed in his right hand. To make fun of him they knelt to him saying, 'Hail, king of the Jews!'. And they spat on him and took the reed and struck him on the head with it. And when they had finished making fun of him, they took off the cloak and dressed him in his own clothes and led him away to crucify him.

Lord, for the times I am disgruntled and complain
about my lot,
Lord, have mercy.
Lord, for the times I mock and ridicule others,
Christ, have mercy.
Lord, for the times I punish others, loading them with
burdens,
Lord, have mercy.

Heal me, Lord, of the injuries I've felt from the words and actions of others.

3 Jesus Falls the First Time

(Hebrews 2: 17–18)

It was essential that he should in this way become completely like his brothers so that he could be a compassionate and trustworthy high priest of God's religion, able to atone for human sins. That is, because he has himself been through temptation he is able to help others who are tempted.

Lord, for the times I have caused others to fall,
Lord, have mercy.
Lord, for the times I fail to show compassion,
Christ, have mercy.
Lord, for the times I am no support to my brothers and sisters,
Lord, have mercy.

Heal me, Lord, of the hurt my pride has suffered. Help me not to be too proud to ask forgiveness of those I have hurt.

4 Jesus Meets his Mother

(Luke 1: 30–33)

'Mary, do not be afraid; you have won God's favour. Listen! You are to conceive and bear a son, and you must name him Jesus. He will be great and will be called Son of the Most High. The Lord God will give him the throne of his ancestor David; he will rule over the House of Jacob for ever and his reign will have no end.'

Lord, for the times I have not accepted your Word
Lord, have mercy.
Lord, for the times I have allowed the troubles and trials of the day to get the better of me.
Christ, have mercy.
Lord, for the times I have been too full of my own importance.
Lord, have mercy.

Lord, heal me of all fear, give me the wisdom to know your will and the strength to carry it out.

5 Simon of Cyrene Helps Jesus to Carry his Cross

(Matthew 27: 32)

On their way out, they came across a man from Cyrene, Simon by name, and enlisted him to carry his cross.

Lord, for the times I fail to help carry other people's burdens,
Lord, have mercy.
Lord, for the times I fail to share whatever you have given me,
Christ, have mercy.
Lord, for the times I do not welcome strangers,
Lord, have mercy.

Lord, heal my lack of openness to others. Help me to make the first move to welcome others.

6 Veronica Wipes the Face of Jesus

(Matthew 25: 35–40)

'For I was hungry and you gave me food; I was thirsty and you gave me drink; I was a stranger and you made me welcome; naked and you clothed me, sick and you visited me, in prison and you came to see me.' Then the virtuous will say to him in reply, 'Lord, when did we see you hungry and feed you; or thirsty and give you drink? When did we see you a stranger and make you welcome; naked and clothe you; sick or in prison and go to see you?' And the King will answer, 'I tell you solemnly, in so far as you did this to one of the least of these brothers of mine, you did it to me.'

Lord, for the times I fail to see you in my neighbour,
Lord, have mercy.
Lord, for the times I fail to show hospitality,
Christ, have mercy.
Lord, for the times I fail to see the needs of others,
Lord, have mercy.

Heal me, Lord, of the prejudices that prevent me from reaching out to others.

7 Jesus Falls the Second Time

(Isaiah 53: 5–6)

Yet he was pierced through for our faults,
crushed for our sins.
On him lies a punishment that brings us peace,
and through his wounds we are healed.

We had all gone astray like sheep,
each taking his own way,
and Yahweh burdened him
with the sins of all of us.

Lord, for the times I have wounded others,
Lord, have mercy.
Lord, for the times I have preferred to go my own way,
Christ, have mercy.
Lord, for the times I have exaggerated the faults of others,
Lord, have mercy.

Heal me, Lord, of all resentments.
Help me to bring your peace and healing to those I have wounded.

8 Jesus Meets the Women of Jerusalem

(Luke 23: 27–28)

Large numbers of people followed him, and of women too, who mourned and lamented for him. But Jesus turned to them and said, 'Daughters of Jerusalem, do not weep for me; weep rather for yourselves and for your children . . .'

Lord, for the times I fail to comfort those in need.
Lord, have mercy.
Lord, for the times I am lacking in generosity.
Christ, have mercy.
Lord, for the times I do not listen to people.
Lord, have mercy.

Lord, fill with your healing love, each moment of my life where there has been a lack of love.
Fill me with your love so that I may share it with others.

9 Jesus Falls the Third Time

(1 Peter 2: 22–24)

He had not done anything wrong, and there had been no perjury in his mouth. He was insulted and did not retaliate with insults; when he was tortured he made no threats but he put his trust in the righteous judge. He was bearing our faults in his own body on the cross, so that we might die to our faults and live for holiness; through his wounds you have been healed. You had gone astray like sheep but now you have come back to the shepherd and guardian of your souls.

Lord, for the times I have accused others falsely,
Lord, have mercy.
Lord, for the times I have been untruthful,
Christ, have mercy.
Lord, for the times I have retaliated unjustly,
Lord, have mercy.

Heal me, Lord, of all insults that have crippled me.
Help me, Lord, to be gentle with others.

10 Jesus is Stripped of his Garments

(John 19: 23–24)

They took his clothing and divided it into four shares, one for each soldier. His undergarment was seamless, woven in one piece from neck to hem; so they said to one another, 'instead of tearing it, let's throw dice to decide who is to have it'. In this way the words of scripture were fulfilled:

"They shared out my clothing among them. They cast lots for my clothes."

Lord, for my immodest thoughts and actions,
Lord, have mercy.
Lord, for the sharpness of my tongue,
Christ, have mercy.
Lord, for my impatience with others,
Lord, have mercy.

Heal me, Lord, of all that I am ashamed. Drive all evil far from me, Lord.

11 Jesus is Nailed to the Cross

(Luke 23: 33–34)

When the reached the place called The Skull, they crucified him there and the two criminals also, one on the right, the other on the left. Jesus said, 'Father, forgive them; they do not know what they are doing.'

Lord, for the times I fail to forgive others,
Lord, have mercy.
Lord, for the times I crucify others,
Christ, have mercy.
Lord, for the times I turn my back on you,
Lord, have mercy.

Heal me, Lord, of all my jealousy, of all that binds and cripples me.

12 Jesus Speaks to his Mother from the Cross

(John 19: 25–27)

Near the cross of Jesus stood his mother and his mother's sister Mary the wife of Clopas, and Mary of Magdala. Seeing his mother and the disciple he loved standing near her, Jesus said to his mother, 'Woman, this is your son'. Then to the disciple he said, 'This is your mother'. And from that moment the disciple made a place for her in his home.

Lord, for the times I do not welcome others into my life,
Lord, have mercy.
Lord, for the times I show disrespect to my mother and father, to my brothers and sisters,
Christ, have mercy.
Lord, for the times I devalue the life you give us,
Lord, have mercy.

Lord, heal my relationships with my parents and family and friends, and with all those with whom I share my life.

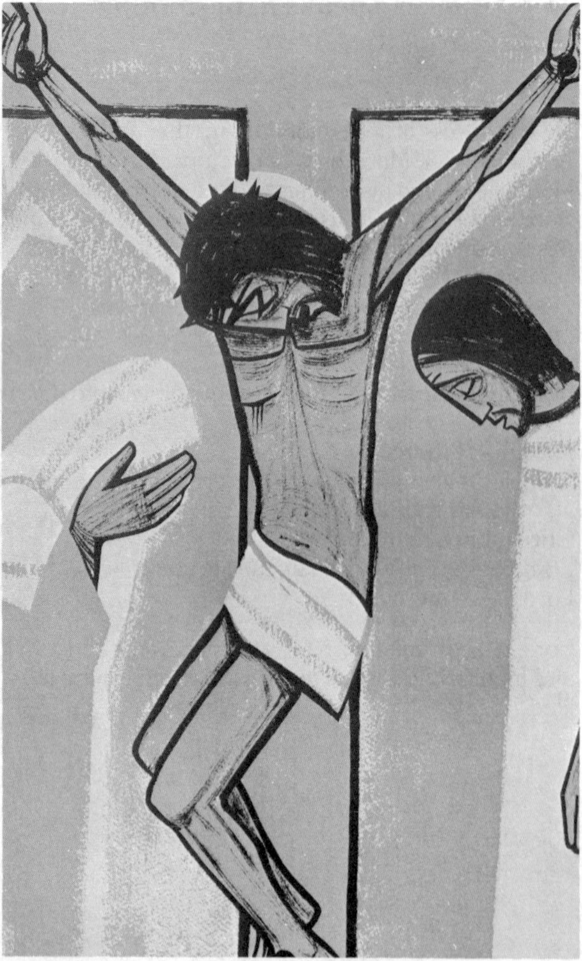

13 Jesus Dies on the Cross

(Luke 23: 44–46)

It was now about the sixth hour and, with the sun eclipsed, a darkness came over the whole land until the ninth hour. The veil of the Temple was torn right down the middle, and when Jesus had cried out in a loud voice, he said, 'Father, into your hands I commit my spirit'. With these words he breathed his last.

Lord, for the times I fail to give myself to you,
Lord, have mercy.
Lord, for the times I fail to commit myself to others,
Christ, have mercy.
Lord, for the times I fail to allow others to be themselves,
Lord, have mercy.

Heal me, Lord, with the power of your Spirit. May you so live in me that I may be used to give new life to those around me.

14 Jesus is Taken Down from the Cross

(John 19:38)

After this, Joseph of Arimathaea, who was a disciple of Jesus – though a secret one because he was afraid of the Jews – asked Pilate to let him remove the body of Jesus. Pilate gave permission, so they came and took it away.

Lord, for the times I fail to turn to you for healing,
Lord, have mercy.
Lord, for the times I fail to admit that I know you,
Christ, have mercy.
Lord, for the times my silence and inaction have offended or misled others,
Lord, have mercy.

Heal me, Lord, of all humiliation. Make of me the person you want me to be.

15 Jesus is Laid in the Tomb

(John 19: 40 42)

They took the body of Jesus and wrapped it with the spices in linen cloths, following the Jewish burial custom. At the place where he had been crucified there was a garden, and in this garden a new tomb in which no one had yet been buried. Since it was the Jewish Day of Preparation and the tomb was near at hand, they laid Jesus there.

Lord, for the times I fail to trust in the power of your resurrection,
Lord, have mercy.
Lord, for the times I fail to respect the thoughts and customs of others,
Christ, have mercy.
Lord, for the times I disturb the peace you came to bring,
Lord, have mercy.

Heal me, Lord, with the peace and joy of your love. Use me to bring your healing to my brothers and sisters.

16 Jesus is Risen

(Mark 16: 14–18)

Lastly, he showed himself to the Eleven themselves while they were at table. He reproached them for their incredulity and obstinacy, because they had refused to believe those who had seen him after he had risen. And he said to them, 'Go out to the whole world; proclaim the Good News to all creation. He who believes and is baptised will be saved; he who does not believe will be condemned. These are the signs that will be associated with believers: in my name they will cast out devils; they will have the gift of tongues; they will pick up snakes in their hands, and be unharmed should they drink deadly poison; they will lay their hands on the sick, who will recover.'

Lord, for the times I fail to spread your Good News,
Lord, have mercy.
Lord, for the times I fail to trust in your promises.
Christ, have mercy.
Lord, for the times that my lack of faith holds me and others from reaching out to you,
Lord, have mercy.

Lord, fill me with the power of your love and the strength to use the gifts you give me.